Yedi Air Fryer Oven XL Cookbook for Beginners

Affordable, Quick and Easy Yedi Air Fryer Oven XL Recipes for Your Air Fryer,

Rotisserie and Dehydrator

Brison Gransh

Table of Contents

Introduction

If you are looking for an advanced multi-functional air fryer oven will make your food rich in taste without adding extra calories. Then Yedi air fryer oven XL is one of the best choices for you. The oven comes with lots of different cooking functions and an extra lager interior to cook whole family food into a single cooking cycle.

The Yedi air fryer oven offers a full set of accessories which helps to make your daily cooking task easy and faster. The company will offer a full set of accessories with all kinds of racks, tray and comes with safety silicon gloves. The fryer is loaded with all advanced cooking features to make your cooking process easy and safe. The oven comes with everything you need and big enough size to feed entire family members. The air fryer oven helps to reduce the number of extra calories from your food and also helps to maintain the crispy, crunchiness of air fried food.

The book contains 80 tasty, delicious, and healthy recipes that come from different categories like breakfast, poultry, beef, pork & lamb, fish & seafood, vegetable& side dishes, snacks, and appetizer, dehydrate, and desserts recipes. The recipes written in this cookbook are unique and written into easily understandable form with their preparation and cooking time followed by step by step cooking instructions. All the recipes written in this book are ends with their exact nutritional value information. The nutritional value information will help you to keep track of daily calorie intake. The book also includes a 30-day meal plan which helps you to track your daily food consumption. This is the first book available in the market on this topic thanks for choosing my cookbook. I hope you love and enjoy all the recipes written in this book.

Chapter 1: Basics of Yedi Air Fryer Oven XL Cookbook

What is Yedi Air Fryer Oven?

Yedi air fryer oven is an advanced cooking machine which comes with extra-large size to cook your whole family food. It is one kind of versatile cooking appliance loaded with 16 different preset cooking functions like Manual, French fries, pizza, wings, chicken steak, fish, shrimp, cake, vegetable, toast, dehydrates, bake, keeps warm and frozen food. The oven comes with 12.7 quarts in size. It works on 1600 watt power to cook your food faster and saves your cooking time.

The Yedi air fryer oven XL comes with lots of accessories which makes daily cooking easy and faster. These accessories include a rotisserie cage, rotisserie rod, drip pan, rotisserie tong, oven rack, skewer rotisserie, rotisserie steak cage, mesh basket, shallow mesh basket, and two mesh trays. The built-in rotisserie allows you to roast whole chicken or turkey. The oven is loaded with safety features like auto shut off. If the oven is on standby mode and you didn't operate it for 60 seconds it will shut-off automatically or if you open the oven door for more than 6 minutes the oven will automatically shut down. The oven comes with a precise and sleek shape and easily fits on your kitchen top.

Initial Test Run before First Use

1. Before starting the initial test run make sure all the stickers, labels, and other packaging materials are removed properly.
2. Remove all the accessories from the oven and clean it using detergent, hot water, and a non-abrasive sponge.
3. Then take a damp cloth and wipe out the interior and exterior parts of the air fryer oven.
4. Then plug the unit into the power supply.
5. First press the ON/OFF button from the control panel. Then press the Menu button and follow the below instructions:
   - Press the Temp/Timer button once and set the temperature at 350° F by

pressing the + and – buttons.

- Again, press the Temp/Timer button to set the time 05 minutes with the help of + and – buttons.

6. Then press the ON/OFF button to start the cooking process for 5 minutes at 350° F temperature. During this process, if any residue is present in the oven will burn out.

7. During this process, you will notice the burning smell but it will vanish after some time.

8. Now your oven is ready to cook your food.

How to Use Yedi Air Fryer Oven?

Yedi air fryer oven is easy to use just select the program as per your recipe needs and start cooking. Follow the step given below.

1. Plug-in Yedi air fryer into a power socket and power it on, the buzzer sound you notice then the digital screen flashes with all the light indicators for few seconds and it shows a blank screen.

2. When you press the ON/OFF touch button the oven screen blinks and light indicators are light up. At this stage, your oven is on standby mode.

3. At the standby mode, only three buttons are in working conditions like Menu, Light, and ON/OFF buttons.

4. To enter into functions press the "Menu" button. Keep pressing the Menu button until you choose the desire cooking function. Remember if the oven is at standby mode and you have not done any operations within 60 seconds the oven will automatically shut down.

5. After selecting the desire function place your food inside the oven and close the oven door then press the ON/OFF button to start the actual cooking process.

6. After finishing the cooking time you will hear a beeping noise and the oven will stop working but you hear the oven fan sound for 1 minute until the oven's internal temperature drops down.

7. Open the door and remove your food from the oven it is ready to serve now.

Control Panel Functions of Yedi Air Fryer Oven XL

The Yedi air fryer oven XL loaded with big size intelligent control panel all the control buttons and functions are given on the panel functions and settings of each function are given as follows.

- Temp/Timer

After selecting the Menu if you want to custom the temperature and time settings this function is used. To set the temperature settings just press the *Temp/Timer* button. The upper display portion blinks now using the + and – button you can set the temperature range between 120° F to 430° F.

If you want to change the time settings Press the *Temp/Timer* button again the bottom half display portion will blink now using the + and – button you can adjust the time settings in between 1 to 60 minutes (while using the Dehydration function you can set up to 8 hours).

- Menu

Using this button you can easily navigate between menu functions. You need to keep pressing the *Menu* button until you select the desire functions given on display. There are 16 preset functions are present on the display menu these functions and their default time and temperature settings are given below.

Function Name	Preset Temperature	Preset Time
Manual	250° F	20 minutes
Cake	360° F	30 minutes
French fries	430° F	20 minutes
Vegetables	400° F	10 minutes
Pizza	350° F	10 minutes
Toast	400° F	05 minutes
Wings	400° F	15 minutes

Dehydrate	160° F	8 hours
Chicken	430° F	25 minutes
Bake	350° F	30 minutes
Steak	400° F	12 minutes
Keep Warm	150° F	30 minutes
Fish	360° F	15 minutes
Defrost	120° F	30 minutes
Shrimp	370° F	10 minutes
Frozen Foods	340° F	20 minutes

- Rotisserie

Using this function you can roast your favorite birds like chicken, turkey, and more. To use this function you need to press the ON/OFF button then the Menu button and last press the rotisserie button. When pressing the Rotisserie button the rotisserie light indicator on it means the function is selected successfully. When you press the ON/OFF button the function will start the cooking process. While using this function you have to need some accessories like Rotisserie Fork, Skewer Rack, steak cage, and rolling cage. Using this function you can roast your favorite chicken more evenly.

- Light Function

You can press this button any time o monitor your cooking process. When you press light function the inside oven light illuminates for 1 minute. The inside light also illuminates when you open the oven door.

- Delay Start Function

Using this function you can suspend the execution process of the selected program for a particular period. Using this function you will get a hot meal ready when you are finishing your work. To use this function you need to press the ON/OFF button then the Menu button and the last Delay Start button. When you press the Delay Start button it shows the delay start default time is 1 hour you can adjust the delay time in the range between 1 minute to 9 hours 59 minutes by pressing the + and – buttons. After setting the time press the ON/OFF button to confirm the delayed start time. The oven starts to count down time to start your cooking process when timer reaches on zero.

- Pause Function

This function is automatically activated when you open the oven door during the cooking process. When you open the oven door all other functions on the control panel are locked and you can only use the ON/OFF button, rotisserie, and light function. If you open the oven door for more than 6 minutes then the oven automatically shut down. When you close the oven door before 6 minutes the oven will automatically continue its current cooking process.

Benefits of Yedi Air Fryer Oven

The air fryer oven comes with various types of benefits some of the important benefits are given as follows:

1. Cook your food in less oil and fats

The air fryer oven is one of the best choices for those people who want to enjoy fried food without worrying about extra calories. As compared with the deep-frying method air fryer uses very little oil and fats to cook your food. Air fryer gives your food a nice crunchy, crispy texture from the outside and makes it tender, juicy from the inside. Cooking your food with less oil and fats means fewer calories intake without compromising the taste and texture like fried food.

2. Loaded with preset functions

The Yedi air fryer comes with 16 preset functions. It allows you to cook your food using various cooking methods in one appliance. While using these preset functions you never need to worry about temperature and time settings. All settings are preset you can also change the preset settings as per recipe needs.

3. Versatile cooking

Yedi air fryer oven is one of the versatile cooking appliance capable to perform different cooking operations like it air frying your food, toast your bread, roast chicken, dehydrate fruits and vegetable slices, broil burgers, make pizza, bake cake and cookies and more. You never need to buy a separate appliance to perform all the tasks. It also saves your kitchen countertop space by performing all these operations into a single appliance.

4. Retain nutritional values

The traditional deep frying method destroys the essential vitamin and nutrition form the food and also creates harmful compounds causes cancer. Yedi air fryer fries your food into very little oil and fats with the help of hot air circulation. In this method of cooking essential vitamins and nutrients are retained in your food without adding bad fats into food.

5. Easy to clean

The Yedi air fryer cooks your food using less oil and fats. Less oil and fat means a lack of oil grease which makes your cleaning process easy. Most of the accessories come with a Yedi air fryer oven is dishwasher safe so it makes your cleaning process very easy.

Cleaning and Maintenance

The following steps guide you on how to clean and maintain your Yedi air fryer after each use.

1. First, unplug the appliance from the power socket and let it cool down at room temperature.
2. Open the oven door and remove all the accessories like an air frying basket, wire rack, drip tray, etc. for cleaning. The accessories come with a Yedi air fryer oven is dishwasher safe. You can clean it in the dishwasher or soak it in soapy water to remove tough stains.
3. Take a soft moist cloth to clean the air fryer oven interior and exterior body. Do not

immerse the oven electrical parts in water. It may cause damage to the appliance and cause fire or electric shock or injury to the person.

4. After finishing the cleaning process make sure all the parts are thoroughly dry. Assemble all the parts and accessories with its original position.

5. Now your Yedi air fryer oven is ready for next use.

Chapter 2: Breakfast

Italian Frittata

Preparation Time: 10 minutes
Cooking Time: 20 minutes
Serve: 4

Ingredients:

- 8 eggs
- 2 small zucchini, chopped and cooked
- 1/2 cup bacon, chopped and cooked
- 1 tbsp fresh parsley, chopped
- 3 tbsp parmesan cheese, grated
- Pepper
- Salt

Directions:

1. Spray a baking dish with cooking spray and set aside.
2. In a bowl, whisk eggs with pepper and salt.
3. Add parsley, cheese, zucchini, and bacon and stir well.
4. Pour egg mixture into the prepared baking dish.
5. Place baking dish on a wire rack in the oven and bake at 350 F for 20 minutes.
6. Serve and enjoy.

Nutritional Value (Amount per Serving):

- Calories 327
- Fat 23.2 g
- Carbohydrates 3.5 g
- Sugar 1.7 g
- Protein 26 g
- Cholesterol 367 mg

Oat Squash Muffins

Preparation Time: 10 minutes
Cooking Time: 20 minutes
Serve: 12

Ingredients:

- 2 eggs
- 1 cup oats
- 1 cup all-purpose flour
- 1 tsp vanilla
- 1/3 cup olive oil
- 1/2 cup yogurt
- 1 tbsp pumpkin pie spice
- 2 tsp baking powder
- 1/2 cup maple syrup
- 1 cup butternut squash puree
- 1/2 tsp sea salt

Directions:

1. Line 12 cups muffin pan with cupcake liners.
2. In a bowl, whisk together eggs, vanilla, oil, yogurt, maple syrup, and squash puree.
3. In a small bowl, mix flour, pumpkin pie spice, baking powder, oats, and salt.
4. Add flour mixture into the wet mixture and stir to combine.
5. Pour batter into the prepared muffin pan.
6. Place muffin pan on a wire rack in the oven and bake at 390 F for 20 minutes.
7. Serve and enjoy.

Nutritional Value (Amount per Serving):

- Calories 171
- Fat 7.1 g

- Carbohydrates 23.8 g
- Sugar 9.4 g
- Protein 3.6 g
- Cholesterol 28 mg

Ham Egg Casserole

Preparation Time: 10 minutes
Cooking Time: 20 minutes
Serve: 2

Ingredients:

- 5 eggs, lightly beaten
- 1/2 cup cheddar cheese, shredded
- 1/3 cup heavy cream
- 2 green onion, chopped
- 1 slice bread, cut into pieces
- 1/3 cup ham, diced
- 1 tbsp pimento, diced
- 1/4 tsp black pepper
- 1/4 tsp salt

Directions:

1. Add bread pieces to the bottom of the greased casserole dish.
2. In a bowl, whisk eggs with heavy cream, pimento, green onion, pepper, and salt.
3. Pour egg mixture over bread. Sprinkle ham and cheese over egg mixture.
4. Place baking dish on a wire rack in the oven and bake at 350 F for 20 minutes.
5. Serve and enjoy.

Nutritional Value (Amount per Serving):

- Calories 413
- Fat 30 g
- Carbohydrates 10.7 g
- Sugar 4.6 g
- Protein 26.3 g
- Cholesterol 479 mg

Banana Bread

Preparation Time: 10 minutes
Cooking Time: 50 minutes
Serve: 10

Ingredients:

- 3 eggs
- 3 bananas
- 1/2 cup walnuts, chopped
- 2 cups almond flour
- 1 tsp baking soda
- 4 tbsp olive oil

Directions:

1. Grease loaf pan with butter and set aside.
2. Add all ingredients except walnut into the food processor and process until combined. Add walnut and stir well.
3. Pour batter into the loaf pan.
4. Place loaf pan on a wire rack in the oven and bake at 350 F for 50 minutes.
5. Slices and serve.

Nutritional Value (Amount per Serving):

- Calories 271
- Fat 21.4 g
- Carbohydrates 13.6 g
- Sugar 4.5 g
- Protein 8.4 g
- Cholesterol 49 mg

Blueberry Oatmeal

Preparation Time: 10 minutes

Cooking Time: 20 minutes

Serve: 6

Ingredients:

- 1 egg
- 1 1/2 cups milk
- 1 cup strawberries, sliced
- 1 cup blueberries
- 2 cups old fashioned oats
- 1 1/2 tsp baking powder
- 1/4 cup maple syrup
- 1/2 tsp salt

Directions:

1. In a bowl, mix oats, salt, and baking powder.
2. Add egg, vanilla, maple syrup, and milk and stir well.
3. Add strawberries and blueberries and stir well.
4. Pour mixture into the greased baking dish.
5. Place baking dish on a wire rack in the oven and bake at 375 F for 20 minutes.
6. Serve and enjoy.

Nutritional Value (Amount per Serving):

- Calories 413
- Fat 18.7 g
- Carbohydrates 53.9 g
- Sugar 14.9 g
- Protein 9.3 g
- Cholesterol 27 mg

Pumpkin Bread

Preparation Time: 10 minutes

Cooking Time: 35 minutes

Serve: 8

Ingredients:

- 2 eggs
- 1/4 cup coconut flour
- 1 tsp pumpkin pie spice
- 1/4 cup chocolate chips
- 1/2 cup pumpkin puree
- 1/4 cup flax seed meal
- 1/4 cup Swerve
- 1 tsp baking powder

Directions:

1. Grease loaf pan with and set aside.
2. Add all dry ingredients into the bowl and mix well. Set aside.
3. In a medium bowl, whisk pumpkin puree and eggs.
4. Pour wet ingredients mixture into the dry ingredients and mix until just combined.
5. Pour batter into the prepared loaf pan.
6. Place loaf pan on a wire rack in the oven and bake at 350 F for 35 minutes.
7. Slice and serve.

Nutritional Value (Amount per Serving):

- Calories 69
- Fat 3.8 g
- Carbohydrates 5.9 g
- Sugar 3.4 g
- Protein 2.6 g
- Cholesterol 42 mg

Baked Egg Muffins

Preparation Time: 10 minutes
Cooking Time: 20 minutes
Serve: 12

Ingredients:

- 12 eggs
- 1/2 cup milk
- 1/4 tsp garlic powder
- 1/2 cup ham, diced
- 1/2 cup cheddar cheese, shredded
- Pepper
- Salt

Directions:

1. Spray 12-cups muffin pan with cooking spray and set aside.
2. In a bowl, whisk eggs with milk, garlic powder, pepper, and salt. Add ham and cheese and stir well.
3. Pour egg mixture into the prepared muffin pan.
4. Place baking dish on a wire rack in the oven and bake at 375 F for 20 minutes.
5. Serve and enjoy.

Nutritional Value (Amount per Serving):

- Calories 114
- Fat 8.8 g
- Carbohydrates 1.2 g
- Sugar 0.7 g
- Protein 7.9 g
- Cholesterol 172 mg

Egg Cheese Casserole

Preparation Time: 10 minutes

Cooking Time: 40 minutes

Serve: 10

Ingredients:

- 12 eggs
- 1/3 cup milk
- 8 oz cheddar cheese, shredded
- 1/4 tsp pepper
- 1 tsp salt

Directions:

1. Spray 9*13-inch casserole dish with cooking spray and set aside.
2. In a bowl, whisk eggs with milk, pepper, and salt. Add shredded cheese and stir well.
3. Pour egg mixture into the prepared casserole dish.
4. Place baking dish on a wire rack in the oven and bake at 350 F for 40 minutes.
5. Serve and enjoy.

Nutritional Value (Amount per Serving):

- Calories 171
- Fat 12.9 g
- Carbohydrates 1.1 g
- Sugar 0.9 g
- Protein 12.6 g
- Cholesterol 221 mg

Tasty Baked Eggs

Preparation Time: 10 minutes
Cooking Time: 45 minutes
Serve: 8

Ingredients:

- 12 eggs
- 16 oz cheddar cheese, shredded
- 1/2 cup all-purpose flour
- 16 oz cottage cheese
- 1 tsp salt

Directions:

1. Grease 9*13-inch baking pan with butter and set aside.
2. In a bowl, whisk eggs with flour, cottage cheese, cheddar cheese, and salt.
3. Pour egg mixture into the prepared baking pan.
4. Place baking pan on a wire rack in the oven and bake at 350 F for 45 minutes.
5. Serve and enjoy.

Nutritional Value (Amount per Serving):

- Calories 402
- Fat 26.5 g
- Carbohydrates 9.3 g
- Sugar 1 g
- Protein 31 g
- Cholesterol 310 mg

Broccoli Quiche

Preparation Time: 10 minutes
Cooking Time: 45 minutes
Serve: 8

Ingredients:

- 2 eggs
- 1/2 cup onion, chopped
- 1 1/2 cups milk
- 1 tsp baking powder
- 2 1/2 cups broccoli, cooked & chopped
- 8 oz cheddar cheese, shredded
- 1 cup flour
- 1 tsp salt

Directions:

1. In a bowl, mix flour, baking powder, and salt and set aside.
2. In a medium bowl, whisk eggs. Add onion and stir well.
3. Pour egg mixture into the flour mixture and stir to combine. Stir in broccoli and cheese.
4. Pour egg mixture into the greased 9-inch pie dish.
5. Place pie dish on a wire rack in the oven and bake at 350 F for 45 minutes.
6. Serve and enjoy.

Nutritional Value (Amount per Serving):

- Calories 225
- Fat 11.7 g
- Carbohydrates 17.5 g
- Sugar 3.1 g
- Protein 12.4 g
- Cholesterol 74 mg

Chapter 3: Poultry

Baked Chicken Breasts

Preparation Time: 10 minutes

Cooking Time: 20 minutes

Serve: 6

Ingredients:

- 6 chicken breasts, skinless & boneless
- 2 tbsp olive oil
- 1/4 tsp pepper
- 1/2 tsp seasoning salt
- 1/4 tsp paprika
- 1 tsp Italian seasoning

Directions:

1. Brush chicken with oil and season with paprika, Italian seasoning, pepper, and salt.
2. Place chicken breasts in a mesh basket.
3. Place mesh basket in the oven and bake at 400 F for 20 minutes.
4. Serve and enjoy.

Nutritional Value (Amount per Serving):

- Calories 320
- Fat 15.7 g
- Carbohydrates 0.2 g
- Sugar 0.1 g
- Protein 42.3 g
- Cholesterol 130 mg

Turkey Meatballs

Preparation Time: 10 minutes
Cooking Time: 25 minutes
Serve: 6

Ingredients:

- 2 eggs
- 2 lbs ground turkey
- 1/2 cup breadcrumbs
- 1 tsp cumin
- 1/2 cup parsley, chopped
- 1/2 cup onion, minced
- 1 tbsp garlic, minced
- 1/2 tsp pepper
- 1 tsp oregano
- 1/2 tsp pepper
- 1 tsp fresh mint, chopped
- 1 tsp salt

Directions:

1. Add all ingredients into the bowl and mix until well combined.
2. Make small balls from the meat mixture and place on a mesh tray and bake at 375 F for 25 minutes.
3. Serve and enjoy.

Nutritional Value (Amount per Serving):

- Calories 362
- Fat 18.7 g
- Carbohydrates 8.8 g
- Sugar 1.2 g
- Protein 44.9 g
- Cholesterol 209 mg

Chicken Patties

Preparation Time: 10 minutes

Cooking Time: 25 minutes

Serve: 4

Ingredients:

- 1 egg
- 1 lb ground chicken
- 1/2 cup mozzarella cheese, grated cheese
- 1 cup carrot, grated
- 1 cup cauliflower, grated
- 1 tsp garlic, minced
- 1/2 cup onion, minced
- 3/4 cup breadcrumbs
- 1/8 tsp pepper
- 3/4 tsp salt

Directions:

1. Add all ingredients into the mixing bowl and mix until well combined.
2. Make patties from meat mixture and place on a mesh tray and bake at 400 F for 25 minutes.
3. Serve and enjoy.

Nutritional Value (Amount per Serving):

- Calories 346
- Fat 11.2 g
- Carbohydrates 20.4 g
- Sugar 3.9 g
- Protein 38.8 g
- Cholesterol 144 mg

Lemon Pepper Chicken

Preparation Time: 10 minutes
Cooking Time: 35 minutes
Serve: 4

Ingredients:

- 4 chicken thighs
- 2 tbsp fresh lemon juice
- 1/2 tsp paprika
- 1 tsp garlic powder
- 1/2 tsp onion powder
- 1 tbsp lemon pepper seasoning
- 2 tbsp olive oil
- 1 tsp salt

Directions:

1. Add chicken to the mixing bowl.
2. Pour lemon juice and olive oil over chicken and coat well.
3. Mix lemon pepper seasoning, paprika, Italian seasoning, onion powder, garlic powder, and salt and rub all over the chicken thighs.
4. Place chicken in baking dish.
5. Place baking dish on a wire rack in the oven and bake at 400 F for 35 minutes.
6. Serve and enjoy.

Nutritional Value (Amount per Serving):

- Calories 184
- Fat 11.6 g
- Carbohydrates 2.1 g
- Sugar 0.5 g
- Protein 17.8 g
- Cholesterol 53 mg

Meatballs

Preparation Time: 10 minutes
Cooking Time: 25 minutes
Serve: 4

Ingredients:

- 1 lb ground chicken
- 1 egg, lightly beaten
- 2 tbsp olive oil
- 1 tbsp parsley, chopped
- 1/2 cup breadcrumbs
- 1/2 cup parmesan cheese, grated
- 1/4 tsp red pepper flakes
- 1/2 tsp dried oregano
- 1 tsp dried onion flakes
- 1 garlic clove, minced
- 1/4 tsp pepper
- 1/2 tsp sea salt

Directions:

1. Add all ingredients into the mixing bowl and mix until well combined.
2. Make balls from the meat mixture and arrange on a mesh tray and bake at 390 F for 25 minutes.
3. Serve and enjoy.

Nutritional Value (Amount per Serving):

- Calories 385
- Fat 19.7 g
- Carbohydrates 11.1 g
- Sugar 1.1 g
- Protein 39.8 g
- Cholesterol 150 mg

Baked Turkey Breast

Preparation Time: 5 minutes

Cooking Time: 45 minutes

Serve: 4

Ingredients:

- 1 lb turkey breast, cut into 1-inch cubes
- 2 tbsp olive oil
- 1 cup mushrooms, cleaned
- 1 tsp garlic powder
- 1/2 lb Brussels sprouts, cut in half
- Pepper
- Salt

Directions:

1. In a small bowl, mix oil, garlic powder, pepper, and salt.
2. In a baking dish, mix turkey, mushrooms, and Brussels sprouts. Pour oil mixture on top.
3. Place baking dish on a wire rack in the oven and bake at 350 F for 45 minutes.
4. Serve and enjoy.

Nutritional Value (Amount per Serving):

- Calories 209
- Fat 9.1 g
- Carbohydrates 11 g
- Sugar 5.7 g
- Protein 22 g
- Cholesterol 49 mg

Dijon Chicken Thighs

Preparation Time: 5 minutes

Cooking Time: 50 minutes

Serve: 4

Ingredients:

- 1 1/2 lbs chicken thighs, skinless and boneless
- 4 tbsp maple syrup
- 2 tsp olive oil
- 2 tbsp Dijon mustard
- 1/4 cup French mustard

Directions:

1. In a bowl, mix maple syrup, olive oil, Dijon mustard, and French mustard.
2. Add chicken to the bowl and mix until chicken is well coated with maple mixture.
3. Arrange chicken in a baking dish.
4. Place baking dish on a wire rack in the oven and bake at 375 F for 50 minutes.
5. Serve and enjoy.

Nutritional Value (Amount per Serving):

- Calories 401
- Fat 15.3 g
- Carbohydrates 13.8 g
- Sugar 12 g
- Protein 49.6 g
- Cholesterol 151 mg

Chili Garlic Chicken Wings

Preparation Time: 5 minutes

Cooking Time: 60 minutes

Serve: 4

Ingredients:

- 2 lbs chicken wings
- 1/2 cup coconut flour
- 1/4 tsp garlic powder
- 1/4 tsp chili powder
- 1/8 tsp paprika
- 2 tsp seasoned salt

Directions:

1. In a bowl, add all ingredients except chicken wings and mix well.
2. Add chicken wings to the bowl and coat well and place on a mesh tray and bake at 400 F for 60 minutes.
3. Serve and enjoy.

Nutritional Value (Amount per Serving):

- Calories 492
- Fat 18.4 g
- Carbohydrates 10.3 g
- Sugar 0.1 g
- Protein 67.7 g
- Cholesterol 202 mg

Chicken Casserole

Preparation Time: 5 minutes
Cooking Time: 15 minutes
Serve: 4

Ingredients:

- 1 lb cooked chicken, shredded
- 1 bell pepper, sliced
- 1/3 cup mayonnaise
- 7 oz cream cheese
- 7 oz shredded cheese
- 2 tbsp tex-mix seasoning
- 1 onion, sliced
- Pepper
- Salt

Directions:

1. Spray a baking dish with butter and set aside.
2. Mix all ingredients except 2 oz shredded cheese in a prepared baking dish. Spread remaining cheese on top.
3. Place baking dish on a wire rack and bake at 400 F for 15 minutes.
4. Serve and enjoy.

Nutritional Value (Amount per Serving):

- Calories 641
- Fat 43.8 g
- Carbohydrates 11.5 g
- Sugar 4.3 g
- Protein 49.7 g
- Cholesterol 199 mg

Tarragon Chicken

Preparation Time: 10 minutes

Cooking Time: 12 minutes

Serve: 2

Ingredients:

- 2 chicken breasts, skinless and boneless
- 1/4 cup dried tarragon
- 1 tbsp butter
- Pepper
- Salt

Directions:

1. Season chicken with pepper and salt and coat with butter.
2. Sprinkle chicken with tarragon and place on a mesh tray and bake at 390 F for 12 minutes.
3. Serve and enjoy.

Nutritional Value (Amount per Serving):

- Calories 339
- Fat 16.8 g
- Carbohydrates 1.8 g
- Sugar 0 g
- Protein 43.1 g
- Cholesterol 145 mg

Chapter 4: Beef, Pork & Lamb

Ranch Pork Chops

Preparation Time: 10 minutes

Cooking Time: 35 minutes

Serve: 4

Ingredients:

- 4 pork chops, boneless
- 4 tbsp olive oil
- 1 1/2 tbsp ranch seasoning

Directions:

1. Mix together ranch seasoning and olive oil and brush over pork chops.
2. Place pork chops in a mesh basket and bake at 400 F for 35 minutes.
3. Serve and enjoy.

Nutritional Value (Amount per Serving):

- Calories 387
- Fat 33.9 g
- Carbohydrates 0 g
- Sugar 0 g
- Protein 18 g
- Cholesterol 69 mg

Meatballs

Preparation Time: 10 minutes

Cooking Time: 20 minutes

Serve: 6

Ingredients:

- 2 lbs ground beef
- 2 tsp coriander
- 1 tsp garlic, minced
- 1 small onion, grated
- 1 tbsp fresh mint, chopped
- 1 egg, lightly beaten
- 1 tsp oregano
- 1 tsp cinnamon
- 2 tsp cumin
- 1/4 cup fresh parsley, minced
- 1/2 tsp allspice
- 1 tsp paprika
- Pepper
- Salt

Directions:

1. Add all ingredients into the large bowl and mix until well combined.
2. Make balls from the meat mixture and place on a mesh tray and bake at 390 F for 20 minutes.
3. Serve and enjoy.

Nutritional Value (Amount per Serving):

- Calories 304
- Fat 10.4 g

- Carbohydrates 2.7 g
- Sugar 10.7 g
- Protein 47.3 g
- Cholesterol 162 mg

Lamb Patties

Preparation Time: 10 minutes
Cooking Time: 8 minutes
Serve: 4

Ingredients:

- 1 lb ground lamb
- 1 tsp dried oregano
- 1 cup feta cheese, crumbled
- 1 tbsp garlic, minced
- 1 jalapeno pepper, minced
- 5 basil leaves, minced
- 10 mint leaves, minced
- 1/4 cup fresh parsley, chopped
- 1/4 tsp pepper
- 1/2 tsp kosher salt

Directions:

1. Add all ingredients into the bowl and mix until well combined.
2. Make patties from meat mixture and place on a mesh tray and bake at 390 F for 8 minutes.
3. Serve and enjoy.

Nutritional Value (Amount per Serving):

- Calories 330
- Fat 16.6 g
- Carbohydrates 5.4 g
- Sugar 1.7 g
- Protein 38.5 g
- Cholesterol 135 mg

Meatballs

Preparation Time: 10 minutes
Cooking Time: 20 minutes
Serve: 8

Ingredients:

- 2 lbs ground beef
- 1/2 cup fresh basil, chopped
- 1/3 cup tomato sauce
- 2 eggs, lightly beaten
- 1 1/2 cups whole wheat breadcrumbs
- 12 oz jar roasted red peppers
- 1/4 cup fresh parsley, chopped
- 1/4 tsp pepper
- 1/2 tsp salt

Directions:

1. Add all ingredients into the large mixing bowl and mix until well combined.
2. Make balls from meat mixture and place on a mesh tray and bake at 350 F for 20 minutes.
3. Serve and enjoy.

Nutritional Value (Amount per Serving):

- Calories 304
- Fat 9.1 g
- Carbohydrates 12.6 g
- Sugar 0.5g
- Protein 38.1 g
- Cholesterol 142 mg

Rosemary Pork Chops

Preparation Time: 10 minutes

Cooking Time: 25 minutes

Serve: 4

Ingredients:

- 4 pork chops, boneless and cut 1/2-inch thick
- 2 garlic cloves, minced
- 1 tsp dried rosemary, crushed
- 1/4 tsp pepper
- 1/4 tsp salt

Directions:

1. Season pork chops with pepper and salt.
2. In a small bowl, mix together garlic and rosemary and rub all over pork chops.
3. Place pork chops on a mesh tray and bake at 350 F for 35 minutes.
4. Serve and enjoy.

Nutritional Value (Amount per Serving):

- Calories 208
- Fat 16 g
- Carbohydrates 0.6 g
- Sugar 0 g
- Protein 14.5 g
- Cholesterol 55 mg

Pork Tenderloin

Preparation Time: 10 minutes
Cooking Time: 35 minutes
Serve: 3

Ingredients:

- 1 lb pork tenderloin
- 1/2 tbsp dried rosemary
- 1 tbsp olive oil
- Pepper
- Salt

Directions:

1. Mix rosemary and olive oil and rub over pork tenderloin.
2. Place pork tenderloin in baking dish.
3. Place baking dish on a wire rack and bake at 400 F for 35 minutes.
4. Remove from oven and season with pepper and salt.
5. Slice and serve.

Nutritional Value (Amount per Serving):

- Calories 258
- Fat 10.1 g
- Carbohydrates 0.4 g
- Sugar 0 g
- Protein 39.6 g
- Cholesterol 110 mg

Tasty Parmesan Pork Chops

Preparation Time: 10 minutes
Cooking Time: 35 minutes
Serve: 4

Ingredients:

- 2 pork chops, boneless
- 1/8 tsp paprika
- 2 tbsp breadcrumbs
- 1/3 cup parmesan cheese, grated
- 1 tbsp olive oil
- 1/4 tsp garlic powder
- 1/2 tsp dried parsley
- Pepper
- Salt

Directions:

1. Spray a baking dish with cooking spray and set aside.
2. Coat pork chops with olive oil.
3. In a shallow dish, mix breadcrumbs, cheese, paprika, parsley, garlic powder, pepper, and salt.
4. Coat pork chops with breadcrumb mixture and place in baking dish.
5. Place baking dish on a wire rack and bake in the oven at 350 F for 35 minutes.
6. Serve and enjoy.

Nutritional Value (Amount per Serving):

- Calories 200
- Fat 15.5 g
- Carbohydrates 2.9 g
- Sugar 0.3 g
- Protein 12.3 g
- Cholesterol 41 mg

Garlic Butter Pork Chops

Preparation Time: 10 minutes
Cooking Time: 15 minutes
Serve: 2

Ingredients:

- 2 pork chops
- 4 tbsp butter, melted
- 2 garlic cloves, minced
- 1 tbsp thyme, chopped
- Pepper
- Salt

Directions:

1. Spray a baking dish with cooking spray and set aside.
2. Season pork chops with pepper and salt and place in a baking dish.
3. Mix butter, thyme, and garlic and pour over pork chops.
4. Place baking dish on a wire rack and bake at 375 F for 15 minutes.
5. Serve and enjoy.

Nutritional Value (Amount per Serving):

- Calories 468
- Fat 43 g
- Carbohydrates 1.9 g
- Sugar 0.1 g
- Protein 18.5 g
- Cholesterol 130 mg

Juicy Pork Chops

Preparation Time: 10 minutes
Cooking Time: 18 minutes
Serve: 2

Ingredients:

- 2 pork chops, boneless
- 1 tsp garlic powder
- 1 tsp onion powder
- 1/2 tbsp paprika
- 1 tbsp olive oil
- 1/2 tsp oregano
- Pepper
- Salt

Directions:

1. Coat pork chops with oil and place in a baking dish.
2. Mix oregano, garlic powder, onion powder, paprika, pepper, and salt and sprinkle over pork chops.
3. Place baking dish on a wire rack and bake in the oven at 400 F for 18 minutes.
4. Serve and enjoy.

Nutritional Value (Amount per Serving):

- Calories 331
- Fat 27.2 g
- Carbohydrates 3.2 g
- Sugar 1 g
- Protein 18.7 g
- Cholesterol 69 mg

Creamy Pork Chops

Preparation Time: 10 minutes
Cooking Time: 60 minutes
Serve: 3

Ingredients:

- 3 pork chops
- 5 oz can cream of mushrooms soup
- 1 cup breadcrumbs
- 2 tbsp flour
- 1/2 tsp garlic powder
- 1/4 cup chicken broth
- 1/2 tbsp Worcestershire sauce
- 1/4 cup milk
- 1 tsp parsley
- 1 egg, lightly beaten

Directions:

1. Spray a baking dish with cooking spray and set aside.
2. Add egg in a shallow dish.
3. In a bowl mix together flour and seasoning.
4. Add breadcrumbs to a plate.
5. Coat pork chops with flour then dip in egg and coat with breadcrumbs and place in baking dish.
6. Place baking dish on a wire rack and bake in the oven at 350 F for 35 minutes.
7. Mix broth, Worcestershire sauce, milk, and soup and pour over pork chops and bake for 25 minutes more.
8. Serve and enjoy.

Nutritional Value (Amount per Serving):

- Calories 480
- Fat 24.6 g
- Carbohydrates 35.8 g
- Sugar 5 g
- Protein 26.9 g
- Cholesterol 126 mg

Chapter 5: Fish & Seafood

Tasty Cajun Shrimp

Preparation Time: 10 minutes
Cooking Time: 10 minutes
Serve: 4

Ingredients:

- 1 lb shrimp, deveined & peeled
- 2 tbsp olive oil
- 3/4 tbsp Cajun seasoning

Directions:

1. Spray a baking dish with cooking spray and set aside.
2. Add shrimp, Cajun seasoning, and oil into the bowl and toss well.
3. Add shrimp into the baking dish.
4. Place baking dish on a wire rack and bake at 350 F for 10 minutes.
5. Serve and enjoy.

Nutritional Value (Amount per Serving):

- Calories 195
- Fat 8.9 g
- Carbohydrates 1.7 g
- Sugar 0 g
- Protein 25.9 g
- Cholesterol 239 mg

Shrimp Casserole

Preparation Time: 10 minutes

Cooking Time: 12 minutes

Serve: 4

Ingredients:

- 1 lb shrimp, peeled and deveined
- 1/4 cup butter, melted
- 2 tbsp white wine
- 1 tbsp garlic, minced
- 2 tbsp fresh parsley, chopped
- 1/2 cup breadcrumbs
- Pepper
- Salt

Directions:

1. Spray a baking dish with cooking spray and set aside.
2. Add shrimp into the mixing bowl. Pour remaining ingredients over shrimp and toss well.
3. Pour shrimp mixture into the baking dish.
4. Place baking dish on a wire rack and bake at 400 F for 12 minutes.
5. Serve and enjoy.

Nutritional Value (Amount per Serving):

- Calories 300
- Fat 14.2 g
- Carbohydrates 12.5 g
- Sugar 1 g
- Protein 28 g
- Cholesterol 269 mg

Garlic Tomato Shrimp

Preparation Time: 10 minutes
Cooking Time: 25 minutes
Serve: 4

Ingredients:

- 1 lb shrimp, peeled
- 2 cups grape tomatoes
- 1 tbsp olive oil
- 1 tbsp garlic, sliced
- Pepper
- Salt

Directions:

1. Spray a baking dish with cooking spray and set aside.
2. Add shrimp, oil, garlic, grape tomatoes, pepper, and salt into the mixing bowl and toss well.
3. Transfer shrimp mixture into the baking dish.
4. Place baking dish on a wire rack and bake at 400 F for 25 minutes.
5. Serve and enjoy.

Nutritional Value (Amount per Serving):

- Calories 184
- Fat 5.6 g
- Carbohydrates 5.9 g
- Sugar 2.4 g
- Protein 26.8 g
- Cholesterol 239 mg

Rosemary Shrimp

Preparation Time: 10 minutes

Cooking Time: 10 minutes

Serve: 4

Ingredients:

- 1 lb shrimp, peeled and deveined
- 1/2 tbsp fresh rosemary, chopped
- 1 garlic clove, minced
- 1 tbsp olive oil
- Pepper
- Salt

Directions:

1. Spray a baking dish with cooking spray and set aside.
2. Add shrimp, rosemary, garlic, oil, pepper, and salt in a mixing bowl and toss well.
3. Pour shrimp mixture into the baking dish.
4. Place baking dish on a wire rack and bake at 400 F for 10 minutes.
5. Serve and enjoy.

Nutritional Value (Amount per Serving):

- Calories 167
- Fat 5.5 g
- Carbohydrates 2.3 g
- Sugar 0 g
- Protein 25.9 g
- Cholesterol 239 mg

Spicy Shrimp

Preparation Time: 10 minutes

Cooking Time: 8 minutes

Serve: 4

Ingredients:

- 1 lb shrimp, peeled and deveined
- 1 tbsp soy sauce
- 3 tbsp butter, melted
- 1 tsp garlic, chopped
- 1 tbsp chili paste

Directions:

1. Spray a baking dish with cooking spray and set aside.
2. Add shrimp into the baking dish.
3. In a bowl, mix together butter, soy sauce, chili paste, and garlic and pour over shrimp and mix well.
4. Place baking dish on a wire rack and bake at 400 F for 8 minutes.
5. Serve and enjoy.

Nutritional Value (Amount per Serving):

- Calories 227
- Fat 11.2 g
- Carbohydrates 3.8 g
- Sugar 1.1 g
- Protein 26.5 g
- Cholesterol 263 mg

Greek Scallops

Preparation Time: 10 minutes
Cooking Time: 15 minutes
Serve: 4

Ingredients:

- 1 1/2 lbs sea scallops
- 4 sun-dried tomatoes, minced
- 2 tbsp olives, chopped
- 8 tbsp butter, melted
- 2 garlic cloves, minced
- 1 tbsp dried basil
- Pepper
- Salt

Directions:

1. Spray a baking dish with cooking spray and set aside.
2. Add all ingredients into the mixing bowl and toss well.
3. Pour scallops mixture into the baking dish.
4. Place baking dish on a wire rack and bake at 400 F for 15 minutes.
5. Serve and enjoy.

Nutritional Value (Amount per Serving):

- Calories 390
- Fat 25.8 g
- Carbohydrates 9.9 g
- Sugar 3.3 g
- Protein 30 g
- Cholesterol 117 mg

Spicy Salmon

Preparation Time: 10 minutes
Cooking Time: 12 minutes
Serve:

Ingredients:

- 4 salmon fillets
- 2 tsp Cajun seasoning
- 4 tbsp brown sugar
- Salt

Directions:

1. Mix together Cajun seasoning, brown sugar, and salt and rub all over salmon.
2. Place salmon on a mesh tray and bake at 390 F for 12 minutes.
3. Serve and enjoy.

Nutritional Value (Amount per Serving):

- Calories 270
- Fat 11 g
- Carbohydrates 8.8 g
- Sugar 8.7 g
- Protein 34.6 g
- Cholesterol 78 mg

Dijon Salmon

Preparation Time: 10 minutes

Cooking Time: 12 minutes

Serve: 4

Ingredients:

- 4 salmon fillets
- 2 tbsp ground Dijon mustard
- 3 tbsp maple syrup

Directions:

1. Arrange salmon fillets on a mesh tray.
2. Mix together Dijon mustard and maple syrup and brush over salmon fillets.
3. Bake salmon fillets at 390 F for 12 minutes.
4. Serve and enjoy.

Nutritional Value (Amount per Serving):

- Calories 282
- Fat 11 g
- Carbohydrates 10.1 g
- Sugar 8.9 g
- Protein 34.5 g
- Cholesterol 78 mg

Baked Lemon Butter Cod

Preparation Time: 10 minutes
Cooking Time: 20 minutes
Serve: 4

Ingredients:

- 1 1/2 lb cod fillet
- 4 garlic cloves, minced
- 2 lemon juice
- 2 tbsp olive oil
- 1 lemon, sliced
- 1/4 cup butter, diced
- Pepper
- Salt

Directions:

1. Place codpieces in the baking dish and season with pepper and salt.
2. Whisk together garlic, lemon juice, and olive oil and pour over cod.
3. Arrange butter pieces and lemon slices on top of cod.
4. Place baking dish on a wire rack and bake at 390 F for 20 minutes.
5. Serve and enjoy.

Nutritional Value (Amount per Serving):

- Calories 309
- Fat 20.3 g
- Carbohydrates 1.7 g
- Sugar 0.6 g
- Protein 30.9 g
- Cholesterol 114 mg

Scallop Gratin

Preparation Time: 10 minutes

Cooking Time: 8 minutes

Serve: 4

Ingredients:

- 1 1/2 lbs sea scallops
- 1 lemon juice
- 1/4 cup white wine
- 1/4 cup cream cheese, softened
- 1/4 cup parmesan cheese, shaved
- 1 tbsp tarragon, chopped
- Pepper
- Salt

Directions:

1. Add scallops to the baking dish.
2. In a bowl, whisk together lemon juice, cream cheese, white wine, tarragon, parmesan cheese, pepper, and salt and pour over scallops.
3. Place baking dish on a wire rack and bake at 390 F for 8 minutes.
4. Serve and enjoy.

Nutritional Value (Amount per Serving):

- Calories 235
- Fat 7.7 g
- Carbohydrates 5.5 g
- Sugar 0.4 g
- Protein 31.6 g
- Cholesterol 76 mg

Chapter 6: Vegetable & Side Dishes

Baked Butternut Squash

Preparation Time: 10 minutes
Cooking Time: 40 minutes
Serve: 4

Ingredients:

- 3 lbs butternut squash, peeled, seeded, and cut into 1-inch cubes
- 1 1/2 tbsp maple syrup
- 1 1/2 tbsp olive oil
- 1/2 tsp cinnamon
- Pepper
- Salt

Directions:

1. In a mixing bowl, toss squash cubes with the remaining ingredients.
2. Spread squash cubes on a mesh tray and bake at 400 F for 40 minutes.
3. Serve and enjoy.

Nutritional Value (Amount per Serving):

- Calories 219
- Fat 5.6 g
- Carbohydrates 45.1 g
- Sugar 12 g
- Protein 3.4 g
- Cholesterol 0 mg

Baked Sweet Potatoes

Preparation Time: 10 minutes

Cooking Time: 40 minutes

Serve: 4

Ingredients:

- 2 large sweet potatoes, cut into 1-inch cubes
- 1/2 tsp chili powder
- 3/4 tsp paprika
- 1 tbsp olive oil
- 1/4 tsp onion powder
- 1/2 tsp garlic powder
- 1/2 tsp cumin
- 1/4 tsp pepper
- 1/2 tsp salt

Directions:

1. In a bowl, toss sweet potatoes with remaining ingredients until well coated.
2. Spread sweet potatoes on a mesh tray and bake at 390 F for 40 minutes.
3. Serve and enjoy.

Nutritional Value (Amount per Serving):

- Calories 94
- Fat 3.8 g
- Carbohydrates 14.9 g
- Sugar 0.5 g
- Protein 1 g
- Cholesterol 0 mg

Baked Carrots

Preparation Time: 10 minutes

Cooking Time: 30 minutes

Serve: 4

Ingredients:

- 24 baby carrots
- 1/4 cup brown sugar
- 1 tsp cinnamon
- 6 tbsp butter, melted
- Pepper
- Salt

Directions:

1. Arrange baby carrots in the baking dish.
2. Pour melted butter over baby carrots.
3. Sprinkle cinnamon, brown sugar, pepper, and salt over baby carrots.
4. Place baking dish on a wire rack and bake at 390 F for 30 minutes.
5. Serve and enjoy.

Nutritional Value (Amount per Serving):

- Calories 210
- Fat 17.4 g
- Carbohydrates 14.3 g
- Sugar 11.7 g
- Protein 0.6 g
- Cholesterol 46 mg

Baked Root Vegetables

Preparation Time: 10 minutes

Cooking Time: 30 minutes

Serve: 4

Ingredients:

- 1 onion, cut into wedges
- 3 medium carrots, cut into 1-inch pieces
- 2 tsp Italian seasoning
- 1 tbsp olive oil
- 1 rutabaga, peeled and cut into 1-inch chunks
- 1 parsnip, cut into 1-inch chunks
- 2 tbsp balsamic vinegar
- Pepper
- Salt

Directions:

1. In a bowl, toss vegetables with remaining ingredients and spread on a mesh tray, and bake at 390 F for 30 minutes.
2. Serve and enjoy.

Nutritional Value (Amount per Serving):

- Calories 128
- Fat 4.5 g
- Carbohydrates 21.3 g
- Sugar 10.7 g
- Protein 2.3 g
- Cholesterol 2 mg

Baked Frozen Vegetables

Preparation Time: 10 minutes
Cooking Time: 30 minutes
Serve: 3

Ingredients:

- 12 oz mixed frozen vegetables
- 1/2 tsp onion powder
- 1/2 tsp garlic powder
- 2 tbsp olive oil
- 1/2 tsp pepper
- 1/2 tsp salt

Directions:

1. In a bowl, toss frozen mixed vegetables with remaining ingredients.
2. Spread vegetables on a mesh tray and bake at 390 F for 30 minutes.
3. Serve and enjoy.

Nutritional Value (Amount per Serving):

- Calories 158
- Fat 9.5 g
- Carbohydrates 15.7 g
- Sugar 3.8 g
- Protein 3.4 g
- Cholesterol 0 mg

Potato Casserole

Preparation Time: 10 minutes
Cooking Time: 60 minutes
Serve: 6

Ingredients:

- 2 eggs
- 8 oz cream cheese, softened
- 1 cup cheddar cheese, shredded
- 10 potatoes, peeled and halved
- 3 tbsp butter
- 1 cup sour cream
- Pepper
- Salt

Directions:

1. Add potatoes to the boiling water and boil for 10 minutes or until tender. Drain well and place in a mixing bowl.
2. Mash the potatoes using masher until smooth.
3. Add remaining ingredients into the mashed potatoes and stir well to combine.
4. Pour potato mixture into the casserole dish
5. Place casserole dish on a wire rack and bake at 325 F for 50 minutes.
6. Serve and enjoy.

Nutritional Value (Amount per Serving):

- Calories 607
- Fat 35 g
- Carbohydrates 58.8 g
- Sugar 4.4 g
- Protein 16.6 g
- Cholesterol 148 mg

Baked Zucchini

Preparation Time: 10 minutes

Cooking Time: 40 minutes

Serve: 8

Ingredients:

- 4 cups zucchini, sliced
- 1 tbsp butter, melted
- 4 eggs, lightly beaten
- 2 cups crushed crackers
- 1 1/2 cup milk
- 2 cups cheddar cheese, shredded

Directions:

1. Spray 9*13-inch casserole dish with cooking spray and set aside.
2. Add sliced zucchini into the casserole dish.
3. In a bowl, whisk together eggs, butter, milk, and 1 cup cheese and pour over sliced zucchini.
4. Sprinkle with crushed crackers and remaining cheese.
5. Place casserole dish on a wire rack and bake at 350 F for 40 minutes.
6. Serve and enjoy.

Nutritional Value (Amount per Serving):

- Calories 251
- Fat 18.8 g
- Carbohydrates 8.7 g
- Sugar 4.1 g
- Protein 12.5 g
- Cholesterol 115 mg

Lemon Baked Potatoes

Preparation Time: 10 minutes

Cooking Time: 60 minutes

Serve: 4

Ingredients:

- 5 potatoes, cut into wedges
- 1/2 cup lemon juice
- 1/3 cup olive oil
- 2 tsp dried oregano
- 3 garlic cloves, minced
- 1 cup of water
- Pepper
- Salt

Directions:

1. Add potato wedges into the 9*13-inch baking dish.
2. In a bowl, whisk together oregano, garlic, lemon juice, oil, water, pepper, and salt, and pour over potatoes.
3. Place baking dish on a wire rack and bake at 325 F for 60 minutes.
4. Serve and enjoy.

Nutritional Value (Amount per Serving):

- Calories 341
- Fat 17.4 g
- Carbohydrates 43.7 g
- Sugar 3.8 g
- Protein 4.9 g
- Cholesterol 43.7 mg

Delicious Paprika Zucchini

Preparation Time: 10 minutes
Cooking Time: 20 minutes
Serve: 2

Ingredients:

- 3 medium zucchinis, cut into chunks
- 1 tsp garlic powder
- 2 tbsp olive oil
- 1 tsp paprika
- Pepper
- Salt

Directions:

1. In a mixing bowl, toss zucchini chunks with paprika, garlic powder, oil, pepper, and salt.
2. Spread zucchini on a mesh tray and bake at 390 F for 15-20 minutes.
3. Serve and enjoy.

Nutritional Value (Amount per Serving):

- Calories 131
- Fat 14.2 g
- Carbohydrates 2.2 g
- Sugar 0.5 g
- Protein 0.9 g
- Cholesterol 0 mg

Zucchini Tomato Bake

Preparation Time: 10 minutes

Cooking Time: 30 minutes

Serve: 6

Ingredients:

- 3 tomatoes, sliced
- 2 yellow squash, sliced
- 2 medium zucchinis, sliced
- 3/4 cup parmesan cheese, shredded
- 1 tbsp olive oil
- Pepper
- Salt

Directions:

1. Spray a 9*13-inch baking dish with cooking spray and set aside.
2. Arrange sliced tomatoes, squash, and zucchinis alternately in the baking dish. Drizzle with olive oil and season with pepper and salt.
3. Sprinkle parmesan cheese on top of vegetables.
4. Place baking dish on a wire rack and bake at 350 F for 30 minutes.
5. Serve and enjoy.

Nutritional Value (Amount per Serving):

- Calories 80
- Fat 5 g
- Carbohydrates 5.5 g
- Sugar 3.1 g
- Protein 4.9 g
- Cholesterol 8 mg

Chapter 7: Snacks & Appetizers

Parmesan Potatoes

Preparation Time: 10 minutes
Cooking Time: 45 minutes
Serve: 4

Ingredients:

- 5 potatoes, cut into wedges
- 2 tbsp lemon juice
- 1/3 cup olive oil
- 2 thyme sprigs
- 1/2 cup parmesan cheese, grated
- 2 garlic cloves, minced
- Pepper
- Salt

Directions:

1. Spray a 9*13-inch baking dish with cooking spray and set aside.
2. Add potato wedges into the baking dish.
3. Mix together lemon juice, oil, garlic, thyme, cheese, pepper, and salt and pour over potatoes and toss well.
4. Place baking dish on a wire rack and bake in the oven at 325 F for 45 minutes.
5. Serve and enjoy.

Nutritional Value (Amount per Serving):

- Calories 374
- Fat 19.7 g
- Carbohydrates 44.3 g
- Sugar 3.3 g
- Protein 8.5 g
- Cholesterol 8 mg

Chicken Dip

Preparation Time: 10 minutes
Cooking Time: 25 minutes
Serve: 8

Ingredients:

- 2 chicken breasts, skinless, boneless, cooked and shredded
- 1 cup Monterey jack cheese, shredded
- 1 cup cheddar cheese, shredded
- 1/4 cup blue cheese, crumbled
- 1/2 cup ranch dressing
- 1/2 cup buffalo wing sauce
- 8 oz cream cheese, softened

Directions:

1. Spray a 1.5-quart casserole dish with cooking spray and set aside.
2. Add cream cheese into the casserole dish and top with shredded chicken, ranch dressing, and buffalo sauce.
3. Sprinkle cheddar cheese, Monterey jack cheese, and blue cheese on top of chicken mixture.
4. Place casserole dish on a wire rack and bake in the oven at 350 F for 25 minutes.
5. Serve and enjoy.

Nutritional Value (Amount per Serving):

- Calories 298
- Fat 22.8 g
- Carbohydrates 2 g
- Sugar 0.6 g
- Protein 20.8 g
- Cholesterol 94 mg

Goat Cheese Dip

Preparation Time: 10 minutes
Cooking Time: 20 minutes
Serve: 8

Ingredients:

- 12 oz goat cheese
- 4 garlic cloves, minced
- 2 tbsp olive oil
- 1/2 cup parmesan cheese, shredded
- 2 tsp rosemary, chopped
- 1 tsp red pepper flakes
- 4 oz cream cheese
- 1/2 tsp salt

Directions:

1. Spray a baking dish with cooking spray and set aside.
2. Add all ingredients into the mixing bowl and mix until well combined.
3. Pour mixture into the baking dish.
4. Place baking dish on a wire rack and bake in the oven at 390 F for 20 minutes.
5. Serve and enjoy.

Nutritional Value (Amount per Serving):

- Calories 294
- Fat 24.9 g
- Carbohydrates 2.3 g
- Sugar 1 g
- Protein 16 g
- Cholesterol 64 mg

Spicy Cheese Dip

Preparation Time: 10 minutes
Cooking Time: 30 minutes
Serve: 10

Ingredients:

- 16 oz cream cheese, softened
- 1/2 cup hot salsa
- 3 cups cheddar cheese, shredded
- 1 cup sour cream

Directions:

1. Spray an 8*8-inch baking dish with cooking spray and set aside.
2. In a mixing bowl, mix together all ingredients until well combined and pour into the baking dish.
3. Place baking dish on a wire rack and bake in the oven at 350 F for 25 minutes.
4. Serve and enjoy.

Nutritional Value (Amount per Serving):

- Calories 348
- Fat 31.9 g
- Carbohydrates 3.4 g
- Sugar 0.7 g
- Protein 12.8 g
- Cholesterol 96 mg

Crab Dip

Preparation Time: 10 minutes
Cooking Time: 15 minutes
Serve: 4

Ingredients:

- 8 oz crab meat
- 1/4 cup onion, chopped
- 1 1/2 tsp garlic, minced
- 1 cup cheddar cheese, shredded
- 1/4 tsp paprika
- 1/2 tsp garlic powder
- 1/2 cup sour cream
- 1/4 cup mayonnaise
- 8 oz cream cheese, softened
- Pepper
- Salt

Directions:

1. Spray a baking dish with cooking spray and set aside.
2. Add all ingredients into the bowl and mix until well combined.
3. Pour mixture into the baking dish.
4. Place baking dish on a wire rack and bake in the oven at 390 F for 15 minutes.
5. Serve and enjoy.

Nutritional Value (Amount per Serving):

- Calories 487
- Fat 41.1 g
- Carbohydrates 9 g
- Sugar 1.7 g
- Protein 19.7 g
- Cholesterol 139 mg

Tasty Broccoli Nuggets

Preparation Time: 10 minutes

Cooking Time: 20 minutes

Serve: 4

Ingredients:

- 1/4 cup almond flour
- 1 cup cheddar cheese, shredded
- 2 cups broccoli florets, cooked until soften
- 2 egg whites
- 1/8 tsp salt

Directions:

1. Add cooked broccoli to the bowl and using masher mash broccoli into small pieces.
2. Add remaining ingredients to the bowl and mix until well combined.
3. Drop 20 scoops of broccoli mixture onto the mesh tray and bake at 350 F for 20 minutes.
4. Serve and enjoy.

Nutritional Value (Amount per Serving):

- Calories 180
- Fat 12.9 g
- Carbohydrates 5 g
- Sugar 1 g
- Protein 11.6 g
- Cholesterol 30 mg

Flavorful Ranch Potatoes

Preparation Time: 10 minutes
Cooking Time: 20 minutes
Serve: 2

Ingredients:

- 1/2 lb baby potatoes, wash and cut in half
- 1/2 tbsp olive oil
- 1/4 tsp dill
- 1/4 tsp chives
- 1/4 tsp paprika
- 1/4 tsp onion powder
- 1/4 tsp garlic powder
- 1/4 tsp parsley
- Salt

Directions:

1. Add all ingredients into the mixing bowl and toss well.
2. Spread potatoes on a mesh tray and bake at 400 F for 20 minutes.
3. Serve and enjoy.

Nutritional Value (Amount per Serving):

- Calories 99
- Fat 3.7 g
- Carbohydrates 14.8 g
- Sugar 0.2 g
- Protein 3.1 g
- Cholesterol 0 mg

Tasty Sweet Potato Fries

Preparation Time: 10 minutes

Cooking Time: 16 minutes

Serve: 2

Ingredients:

- 2 sweet potatoes, peeled and cut into fries shape
- 1/4 tsp chili powder
- 1 tbsp olive oil
- Salt

Directions:

1. In a mixing bowl, add sweet potato fries, chili powder, garlic powder, olive oil, and salt and toss until well coated.
2. Arrange sweet potato fries on a mesh tray and bake at 380 F for 16 minutes.
3. Serve and enjoy.

Nutritional Value (Amount per Serving):

- Calories 238
- Fat 7.3 g
- Carbohydrates 42 g
- Sugar 0.8 g
- Protein 2.3 g
- Cholesterol 0 mg

Sweet Chickpeas

Preparation Time: 10 minutes
Cooking Time: 12 minutes
Serve: 4

Ingredients:

- 14 oz can chickpeas, rinsed, drained and pat dry
- 1 tbsp olive oil
- 1/2 tsp ground cinnamon
- 1 tbsp maple syrup
- Pepper
- Salt

Directions:

1. Spread chickpeas on a mesh tray and bake at 390 F for 12 minutes.
2. In a large bowl, mix together cinnamon, maple syrup, oil, pepper, and salt. Add chickpeas and toss well.
3. Serve and enjoy.

Nutritional Value (Amount per Serving):

- Calories 170
- Fat 4.7 g
- Carbohydrates 27.6 g
- Sugar 3 g
- Protein 5.3 g
- Cholesterol 0 mg

Parmesan Carrot Fries

Preparation Time: 10 minutes
Cooking Time: 15 minutes
Serve: 4

Ingredients:

- 4 carrots, peeled and cut into fries
- 2 tbsp parmesan cheese, grated
- 1 1/2 tbsp garlic, minced
- 2 tbsp olive oil
- Pepper
- Salt

Directions:

1. Add carrots and remaining ingredients into the mixing bowl and toss well.
2. Add carrots fries on a mesh tray and bake at 350 F for 15 minutes.
3. Serve and enjoy.

Nutritional Value (Amount per Serving):

- Calories 99
- Fat 7.6 g
- Carbohydrates 7.2 g
- Sugar 3 g
- Protein 1.6 g
- Cholesterol 2 mg

Chapter 8: Dehydrate

Lemon Slices

Preparation Time: 10 minutes
Cooking Time: 10 hours
Serve: 4

Ingredients:

- 4 lemons, wash and cut into 1/4-inch thick slices

Directions:

1. Arrange lemon slices on the mesh trays and insert them in the oven.
2. Cook on DEHYDRATE mode at 125 F for 10 hours.

Nutritional Value (Amount per Serving):

- Calories 17
- Fat 0.2 g
- Carbohydrates 5.4 g
- Sugar 1.5 g
- Protein 0.6 g
- Cholesterol 0 mg

Parsnips Chips

Preparation Time: 10 minutes

Cooking Time: 6 hours

Serve: 2

Ingredients:

- 1 parsnip, cut into 1/4-inch thick slices

Directions:

1. Arrange parsnip slices on the mesh trays and insert them in the oven.
2. Cook on DEHYDRATE mode at 125 F for 6 hours.
3. Store parsnip chips in an airtight container.

Nutritional Value (Amount per Serving):

- Calories 50
- Fat 0.2 g
- Carbohydrates 12 g
- Sugar 3.2 g
- Protein 0.8 g
- Cholesterol 0 mg

Eggplant Chips

Preparation Time: 10 minutes
Cooking Time: 4 hours
Serve: 4

Ingredients:

- 1 eggplant, cut into 1/4-inch thick slices
- 1 tsp paprika

Directions:

1. Arrange eggplant slices on the mesh trays and sprinkle with paprika and insert in the oven.
2. Cook on DEHYDRATE mode at 145 F for 4 hours.

Nutritional Value (Amount per Serving):

- Calories 30
- Fat 0.3 g
- Carbohydrates 7 g
- Sugar 3.5 g
- Protein 1.2 g
- Cholesterol 0 mg

Beet Chips

Preparation Time: 10 minutes

Cooking Time: 8 hours

Serve: 4

Ingredients:

- 4 medium beets, peel and sliced

Directions:

1. Arrange beet slices on the mesh trays and insert them in the oven.
2. Cook on DEHYDRATE mode at 135 F for 8 hours.

Nutritional Value (Amount per Serving):

- Calories 44
- Fat 0.2 g
- Carbohydrates 10 g
- Sugar 8 g
- Protein 1.7 g
- Cholesterol 0 mg

Cucumber Chips

Preparation Time: 10 minutes

Cooking Time: 6 hours

Serve: 4

Ingredients:

- 1 large cucumber, sliced
- 1/8 tsp pepper
- 1/4 tsp salt

Directions:

1. Arrange cucumber slices on the mesh trays and season with pepper and salt and insert in the oven.
2. Cook on DEHYDRATE mode at 135 F for 6 hours.

Nutritional Value (Amount per Serving):

- Calories 11
- Fat 0.1 g
- Carbohydrates 2.8 g
- Sugar 1.3 g
- Protein 0.5 g
- Cholesterol 0 mg

Green Apple Slices

Preparation Time: 10 minutes

Cooking Time: 8 hours

Serve: 4

Ingredients:

- 2 green apple, cored and cut into 1/8-inch thick slices

Directions:

1. Arrange green apple slices on the mesh trays and insert them in the oven.
2. Cook on DEHYDRATE mode at 145 F for 8 hours.

Nutritional Value (Amount per Serving):

- Calories 59
- Fat 0.2 g
- Carbohydrates 15.9 g
- Sugar 11.6 g
- Protein 0.3 g
- Cholesterol 0 mg

Zucchini Chips

Preparation Time: 10 minutes
Cooking Time: 8 hours
Serve: 4

Ingredients:

- 2 zucchini, cut into 1/4-inch thick slices
- 1 tsp olive oil
- Pepper
- Salt

Directions:

1. Toss zucchini slices with oil, pepper, and salt in a bowl.
2. Arrange zucchini slices on the mesh trays and insert them in the oven.
3. Cook on DEHYDRATE mode at 135 F for 8 hours.

Nutritional Value (Amount per Serving):

- Calories 26
- Fat 1.4 g
- Carbohydrates 3.3 g
- Sugar 1.7 g
- Protein 1.2 g
- Cholesterol 0 mg

Cinnamon Apple Slices

Preparation Time: 10 minutes
Cooking Time: 8 hours
Serve: 4

Ingredients:

- 2 apples, cut into 1/8-inch thick slices
- 1 tsp ground cinnamon

Directions:

1. Arrange apple slices on the mesh trays and sprinkle with cinnamon and insert in the oven.
2. Cook on DEHYDRATE mode at 135 F for 8 hours.

Nutritional Value (Amount per Serving):

- Calories 59
- Fat 0.2 g
- Carbohydrates 15.9 g
- Sugar 11.6 g
- Protein 0.3 g
- Cholesterol 0 mg

Banana Slices

Preparation Time: 10 minutes

Cooking Time: 6 hours

Serve: 2

Ingredients:

- 2 bananas, peel & cut into 1/8-inch thick slices

Directions:

1. Arrange banana slices on the mesh trays and insert them in the oven.
2. Cook on DEHYDRATE mode at 135 F for 6 hours.

Nutritional Value (Amount per Serving):

- Calories 105
- Fat 0.4 g
- Carbohydrates 27 g
- Sugar 14.4 g
- Protein 1.3 g
- Cholesterol 0 mg

Pear Slices

Preparation Time: 10 minutes

Cooking Time: 5 hours

Serve: 4

Ingredients:

- 2 pears, cut into 1/4-inch thick slices

Directions:

1. Arrange pear slices on the mesh trays and insert them in the oven.
2. Cook on DEHYDRATE mode at 160 F for 5 hours.

Nutritional Value (Amount per Serving):

- Calories 60
- Fat 0.2 g
- Carbohydrates 15.9 g
- Sugar 10.2 g
- Protein 0.4 g
- Cholesterol 0 mg

Chapter 9: Desserts

Baked Apples

Preparation Time: 10 minutes

Cooking Time: 10 minutes

Serve: 6

Ingredients:

- 4 apples, sliced
- 2 tbsp butter, melted
- 1 tsp apple pie spice
- 1/2 cup erythritol

Directions:

1. Add apple slices in a large bowl and sprinkle with sweetener and apple pie spice.
2. Add melted butter and toss to coat.
3. Transfer apple slices in a baking dish.
4. Place baking dish on a wire rack and bake at 350 F for 10 minutes.
5. Serve and enjoy.

Nutritional Value (Amount per Serving):

- Calories 73
- Fat 4.6 g
- Carbohydrates 8.2 g
- Sugar 5.4 g
- Protein 0 g
- Cholesterol 0 mg

Cream Cheese Muffins

Preparation Time: 10 minutes
Cooking Time: 16 minutes
Serve: 10

Ingredients:

- 2 eggs
- 1 tsp ground cinnamon
- 1/2 tsp vanilla
- 1/2 cup erythritol
- 8 oz cream cheese

Directions:

1. In a bowl, mix together cream cheese, vanilla, erythritol, and eggs until soft.
2. Pour batter into the silicone muffin molds and sprinkle cinnamon on top.
3. Place muffin molds on a wire rack and bake at 325 F for 16 minutes.
4. Serve and enjoy.

Nutritional Value (Amount per Serving):

- Calories 90
- Fat 8.8 g
- Carbohydrates 13 g
- Sugar 12.2 g
- Protein 2.8 g
- Cholesterol 58 mg

Blueberry Muffins

Preparation Time: 10 minutes
Cooking Time: 20 minutes
Serve: 12

Ingredients:

- 3 large eggs
- 2 1/2 cups almond flour
- 3/4 cup blueberries
- 1/3 cup coconut oil, melted
- 1 1/2 tsp baking powder
- 1/2 cup erythritol
- 1/2 tsp vanilla
- 1/3 cup almond milk

Directions:

1. In a large bowl, mix together almond flour, baking powder, erythritol.
2. Stir in the coconut oil, vanilla, eggs, and almond milk.
3. Add blueberries and fold well.
4. Pour batter into the silicone muffin molds.
5. Place molds on a wire rack and bake at 325 F for 20 minutes.
6. Serve and enjoy.

Nutritional Value (Amount per Serving):

- Calories 215
- Fat 19 g
- Carbohydrates 5 g
- Sugar 2 g
- Protein 7 g
- Cholesterol 45 mg

Coconut Pie

Preparation Time: 10 minutes

Cooking Time: 12 minutes

Serve: 6

Ingredients:

- 2 eggs
- 1 1/2 tsp vanilla
- 1/2 cup coconut flour
- 1/2 cup Swerve
- 1 cup shredded coconut
- 1/4 cup butter
- 1 1/2 cups coconut milk

Directions:

1. Spray a 6-inch baking dish with cooking spray and set aside.
2. Add all ingredients into the large bowl and mix until well combined.
3. Pour batter into the prepared dish.
4. Place baking dish on a wire rack and bake at 350 F for 12 minutes.
5. Slice and serve.

Nutritional Value (Amount per Serving):

- Calories 317
- Fat 28.9 g
- Carbohydrates 32.3 g
- Sugar 23.1 g
- Protein 5.1 g
- Cholesterol 75 mg

Chocolate Brownies

Preparation Time: 10 minutes
Cooking Time: 35 minutes
Serve: 9

Ingredients:

- 2 eggs
- 2/3 cup unsweetened cocoa powder
- 2 avocados, mashed
- 2 tbsp swerve
- 1 tsp baking powder
- 4 tbsp coconut oil, melted
- 1/3 cup chocolate chips, melted

Directions:

1. In a mixing bowl, mix together all dry ingredients.
2. In a medium bowl, mix together avocado and eggs until well combined.
3. Add dry mixture to the wet along with melted chocolate and oil. Mix well.
4. Pour batter into a baking dish.
5. Place baking dish on a wire rack and bake at 325 F for 35 minutes.
6. Slice and serve.

Nutritional Value (Amount per Serving):

- Calories 207
- Fat 18 g
- Carbohydrates 11 g
- Sugar 3.6 g
- Protein 3.8 g
- Cholesterol 38 mg

Pumpkin Cookies

Preparation Time: 10 minutes
Cooking Time: 25 minutes
Serve: 25

Ingredients:

- 1 egg
- 1 tsp vanilla
- 1/2 cup butter
- 1/2 cup pumpkin puree
- 2 cups almond flour
- 1 tsp liquid stevia
- 1/2 tsp pumpkin pie spice
- 1/2 tsp baking powder

Directions:

1. In a large bowl, add all ingredients and mix until well combined.
2. Make 25 cookies from the mixture and place them onto a mesh tray and bake at 320 F for 25 minutes.
3. Serve and enjoy.

Nutritional Value (Amount per Serving):

- Calories 46
- Fat 4.6 g
- Carbohydrates 0.9 g
- Sugar 0.3 g
- Protein 0.7 g
- Cholesterol 15 mg

Raspberry Cobbler

Preparation Time: 10 minutes

Cooking Time: 10 minutes

Serve: 6

Ingredients:

- 1 egg, lightly beaten
- 1 cup raspberries, sliced
- 2 tsp swerve
- 1/2 tsp vanilla
- 1 tbsp butter, melted
- 1 cup almond flour

Directions:

1. Add raspberries to the baking dish.
2. Sprinkle sweetener over raspberries.
3. Mix together almond flour, vanilla, and butter in the bowl.
4. Add egg in almond flour mixture and stir well to combine.
5. Spread almond flour mixture over sliced raspberries.
6. Place baking dish on a wire rack and bake at 350 F for 10 minutes.
7. Serve and enjoy.

Nutritional Value (Amount per Serving):

- Calories 66
- Fat 5 g
- Carbohydrates 3 g
- Sugar 1 g
- Protein 2 g
- Cholesterol 32 mg

Almond Muffins

Preparation Time: 10 minutes
Cooking Time: 20 minutes
Serve: 12

Ingredients:

- 4 eggs
- 1 tsp baking soda
- 1 orange zest
- 1 orange juice
- 1/2 cup butter, melted
- 3 cups almond flour

Directions:

1. Line 12-cups muffin tin with cupcake liners and set aside.
2. Add all ingredients into the large bowl and mix until well combined.
3. Pour mixture into the prepared muffin tin.
4. Place muffin tin on a wire rack and bake at 350 F for 20 minutes.
5. Serve and enjoy.

Nutritional Value (Amount per Serving):

- Calories 273
- Fat 24 g
- Carbohydrates 6 g
- Sugar 1 g
- Protein 2 g
- Cholesterol 75 mg

Moist Peanut Butter Muffins

Preparation Time: 10 minutes
Cooking Time: 20 minutes
Serve: 12

Ingredients:

- 1 cup peanut butter
- 1/2 cup maple syrup
- 1 tsp baking soda
- 1 tsp vanilla
- 1/2 cup of cocoa powder
- 1 cup applesauce

Directions:

1. Line 12-cups muffin tin with cupcake liners and set aside.
2. Add all ingredients into the blender and blend until smooth.
3. Pour blended mixture into the prepared muffin tin.
4. Place muffin tin on a wire rack and bake at 350 F for 20 minutes.
5. Serve and enjoy.

Nutritional Value (Amount per Serving):

- Calories 178
- Fat 11.3 g
- Carbohydrates 17.3 g
- Sugar 12 g
- Protein 6.1 g
- Cholesterol 0 mg

Peanut Butter Cake

Preparation Time: 10 minutes
Cooking Time: 30 minutes
Serve: 8

Ingredients:

- 1 1/2 cups all-purpose flour
- 1/2 cup peanut butter powder
- 1 tsp vanilla
- 1 tbsp apple cider vinegar
- 1/3 cup vegetable oil
- 1 tsp baking soda
- 1 cup of water
- 1 cup of sugar
- 1/2 tsp salt

Directions:

1. In a large mixing bowl, mix together flour, baking soda, peanut butter powder, sugar, and salt.
2. In a small bowl, whisk together oil, vanilla, vinegar, and water.
3. Pour oil mixture into the flour mixture and stir until well combined.
4. Pour batter into the greased cake pan.
5. Place cake pan on a wire rack and bake at 350 F for 30 minutes.
6. Slice and serve.

Nutritional Value (Amount per Serving):

- Calories 264
- Fat 1.8 g
- Carbohydrates 43.2 g
- Sugar 25.3 g
- Protein 2.6 g
- Cholesterol 0 mg

Chapter 10: 30-Day Meal Plan

Day 1

Breakfast- Italian Frittata

Lunch- Tasty Cajun Shrimp

Dinner- Chili Garlic Chicken Wings

Day 2

Breakfast- Broccoli Quiche

Lunch- Shrimp Casserole

Dinner- Chicken Casserole

Day 3

Breakfast- Italian Frittata

Lunch- Garlic Tomato Shrimp

Dinner- Tarragon Chicken

Day 4

Breakfast- Broccoli Quiche

Lunch- Rosemary Shrimp

Dinner- Ranch Pork Chops

Day 5

Breakfast- Tasty Baked Eggs

Lunch- Spicy Shrimp

Dinner- Lamb Patties

Day 6

Breakfast- Egg Cheese Casserole

Lunch- Greek Scallops

Dinner- Rosemary Pork Chops

Day 7

Breakfast- Baked Egg Muffins

Lunch- Spicy Salmon

Dinner- Pork Tenderloin

Day 8

Breakfast- Pumpkin Bread

Lunch- Dijon Salmon

Dinner- Rosemary Pork Chops

Day 9

Breakfast- Blueberry Oatmeal

Lunch- Baked Lemon Butter Cod

Dinner- Tasty Parmesan Pork Chops

Day 10

Breakfast- Ham Egg Casserole

Lunch- Scallop Gratin

Dinner- Pork Tenderloin

Day 11

Breakfast- Banana Bread

Lunch- Baked Chicken Breasts

Dinner- Tasty Parmesan Pork Chops

Day 12

Breakfast- Oat Squash Muffins

Lunch- Chicken Patties

Dinner- Garlic Butter Pork Chops

Day 13

Breakfast- Ham Egg Casserole

Lunch- Lemon Pepper Chicken

Dinner- Juicy Pork Chops

Day 14

Breakfast- Italian Frittata

Lunch- Baked Turkey Breast

Dinner- Tasty Parmesan Pork Chops

Day 15

Breakfast- Oat Squash Muffins

Lunch- Dijon Chicken Thighs

Dinner- Creamy Pork Chops

Day 16

Breakfast- Italian Frittata

Lunch- Tasty Cajun Shrimp

Dinner- Chili Garlic Chicken Wings

Day 17

Breakfast- Broccoli Quiche

Lunch- Shrimp Casserole

Dinner- Chicken Casserole

Day 18

Breakfast- Italian Frittata

Lunch- Garlic Tomato Shrimp

Dinner- Tarragon Chicken

Day 19

Breakfast- Broccoli Quiche

Lunch- Rosemary Shrimp

Dinner- Ranch Pork Chops

Day 20

Breakfast- Tasty Baked Eggs

Lunch- Spicy Shrimp

Dinner- Lamb Patties

Day 21

Breakfast- Egg Cheese Casserole

Lunch- Greek Scallops

Dinner- Rosemary Pork Chops

Day 22

Breakfast- Baked Egg Muffins

Lunch- Spicy Salmon

Dinner- Pork Tenderloin

Day 23

Breakfast- Pumpkin Bread

Lunch- Dijon Salmon

Dinner- Rosemary Pork Chops

Day 24

Breakfast- Blueberry Oatmeal

Lunch- Baked Lemon Butter Cod

Dinner- Tasty Parmesan Pork Chops

Day 25

Breakfast- Ham Egg Casserole

Lunch- Scallop Gratin

Dinner- Pork Tenderloin

Day 26

Breakfast- Banana Bread

Lunch- Baked Chicken Breasts

Dinner- Tasty Parmesan Pork Chops

Day 27

Breakfast- Oat Squash Muffins

Lunch- Chicken Patties

Dinner- Garlic Butter Pork Chops

Day 28

Breakfast- Ham Egg Casserole

Lunch- Lemon Pepper Chicken

Dinner- Juicy Pork Chops

Day 29

Breakfast- Italian Frittata

Lunch- Baked Turkey Breast

Dinner- Tasty Parmesan Pork Chops

Day 30

Breakfast- Oat Squash Muffins

Lunch- Dijon Chicken Thighs

Dinner- Creamy Pork Chops

Conclusion

Then Yedi air fryer oven XL is one of the best choices for you. The oven comes with lots of different cooking functions and an extra lager interior to cook whole family food into a single cooking cycle.

The book contains 80 tasty, delicious, and healthy recipes that come from different categories like breakfast, poultry, beef, pork & lamb, fish & seafood, vegetable& side dishes, snacks, and appetizer, dehydrate, and desserts recipes. The recipes written in this cookbook are unique and written into easily understandable form with their preparation and cooking time followed by step by step cooking instructions. All the recipes written in this book are ends with their exact nutritional value information.

Printed in Great Britain
by Amazon

64972063R00061